Album
of
Dogs

Album of Dogs

BY MARGUERITE HENRY

Illustrated by Wesley Dennis

RAND McNALLY & COMPANY

CHICAGO · NEW YORK · SAN FRANCISCO

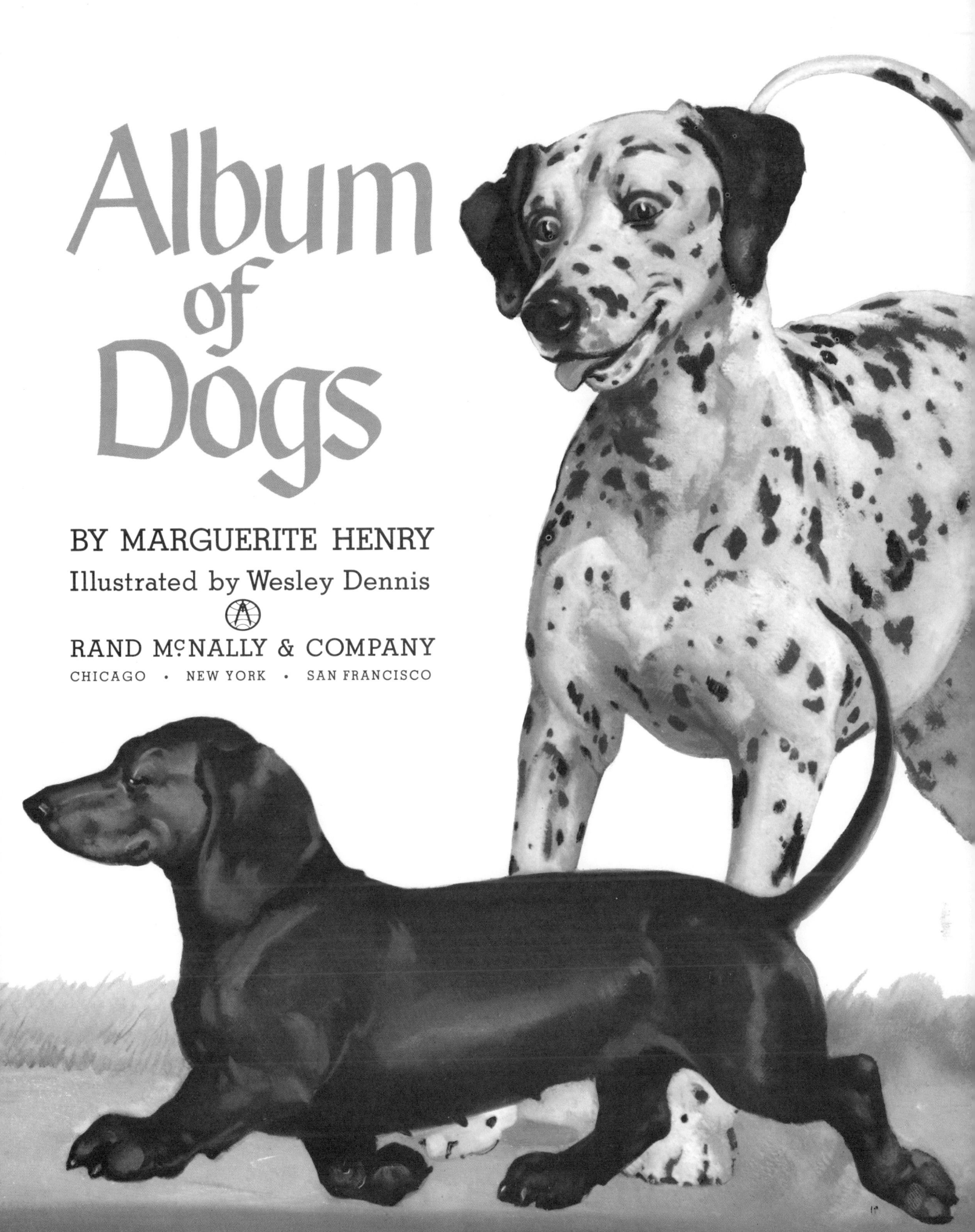

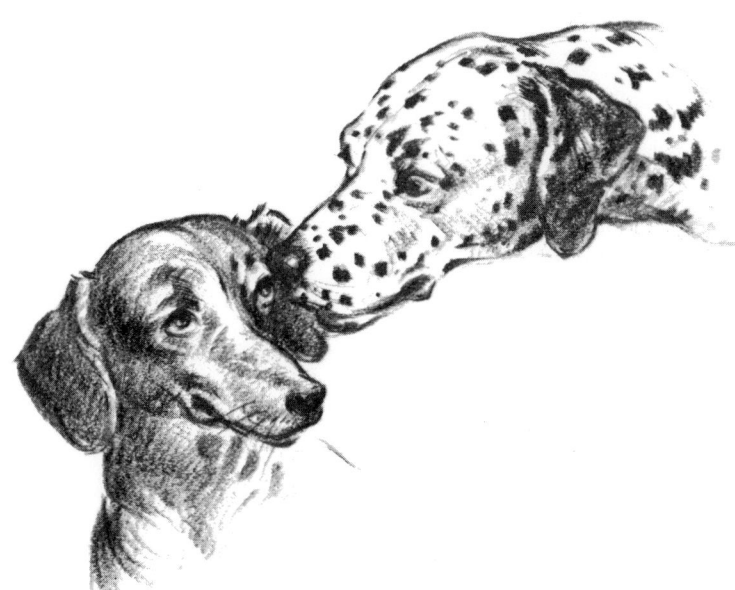

To Alexander
the mole digger

And to the memory of Dice—
who was clean but not spotless

Contents

Index of Breeds

Album
of
Dogs

The Scot's Collie Dog

BONNIE WAS HER NAME, and lovely as it was, it did not begin to describe the golden glory of her coat or the whiteness of the ruff that framed her gentle face.

Bonnie's master was a Scotch Highlander, a Mister Peebles, who was as old and gnarled as the walking stick he carried. In all Scotland there was no better man with a Collie. He had trained Bonnie not only to sort and cull sheep, but also to drive a new flock home alone. And then to pen them all by herself.

So well did Bonnie understand Mister Peebles that her mind seemed to dart ahead of his. Whenever he pinned his purse to his belt and she heard the coins jingle, her whole being quivered in expectancy, "Another new flock for me to drive home?"

One such day the two of them set off in high spirits for a neighboring town. There Mister Peebles examined some black-legged, fine-wooled sheep and found them to be to his liking. Even as he parted with his silver, his face never lost its glow of pleasure.

"Now, gurrl," he waved to Bonnie, "away ye go—acrost the moor and home—with the finest flock in the kingdom!"

Bonnie took command at once. She crept in slowly amongst the flock to single out the leader. Then she stared at him in a way that plainly said, "You are still the leader, but I will show the way."

Mister Peebles watched a moment, happy in knowing that Bonnie would drive the sheep while pretending to follow. And if any maverick so much as made a dash for freedom, she would ride on his back if necessary to bring him into the flock.

When Bonnie and the sheep were lost to sight in a dip of the hills, the master turned his footsteps toward the village pub for an hour of pleasantry. Comfortably settled with a glass of ale in his hand, he toasted his Collie, boasting to every ear that would listen, "Aye, mon, my Bonnie outshines all others e'en as the moon outshines the stars."

Late that afternoon old Mister Peebles tottered home, fully expecting to find Bonnie on watch over the new flock. But she was not there. Nor were the sheep.

"Kate! Kate!" he bellowed into the house. "Where's my Bonnie?"

His wife came running, wiping her hands on her apron. "There, there, Mister Peebles. It's nae good meetin' trouble. Bonnie'll be here soon, and the sheep, too—wagging their stubby tails behind 'em!"

Like a good drover herself, Mistress Peebles nudged her man into the house and settled him down to a bowl of porridge and a nap afterward.

An hour slid by, and another. A yellow moon came up over the hills. Now alarmed herself, Mistress Peebles shook her husband awake. "Bonnie didna' come!" she wailed. "Could it be she's deep drooned in the running stream?"

The old man leaped from sleep. His mind was confused. Had he been dreaming? Had he really bought black-legged sheep with wool so fine? And where, oh where was his Bonnie?

Grabbing his walking stick, he ran out into the night, crying, "Bonnie! Bonnie!"

He groped past the empty sheepfold, stumbling down the hillside, peering this way and that into the darkness. A tatter of

mist seemed to rise up from the stream. Or was it a gray fog of sheep? He squinted into it; he thought he saw something move. Then a lamb blatted, and a ewe baa-aa-ed in reply, and a whole chorus of blattings and baa-aa-ings filled the night. And there, in a shaft of moonlight, he caught sight of Bonnie's snow-white ruff!

Forgetting his years, he scrambled up the hill to the sheepfold and threw wide the gate. "Guid gur-r-r-l!" he panted as his Bonnie herded the flock into the fold. "Verra guid g . . ."

Suddenly his voice broke in his throat. What was that flopping thing she carried in her mouth? A dead hare? A dead squirrel? And then he saw it for what it was—a live pup! "Och, Bonnie!" he cried. "Och, Bonnie! Well did I know ye were going to have little ones. But, O, m'lass, how could I guess 'twould be this day?"

With great tenderness he took her pup and tucked it into his knitted waistcoat for warmth. Then he stooped down to touch Bonnie's head, but she was off, streaking away into the mist.

Once, twice, and a third time that night she returned, carrying another pup and another and another until all were gathered in the cottage kitchen. When at last she settled down to nurse, Mister Peebles knelt beside her, his knees cracking, his voice sobbing. Shamelessly he let the hot tears fall. "My Bonnie lass," he said very softly, "canst ye e'er forgive me? It aches me," he said, stroking the dirt-matted coat, "to think I made ye drive the sheep whilst ye had little ones to whelp!"

Bonnie wriggled her family into position and looked up at her master. Her honest eyes said, "There is nothing to forgive. Nothing at all. I durst not for my life leave the flock." Then she licked each of her puppies in turn and, satisfied at last, dropped off to sleep.

The story of Bonnie is a true one. It probably happened before, and may again—wherever there are flocks of sheep and Scot's Collie dogs to tend them.

Why the name Collie? you ask. "A moot question," say the Scotch shepherds. They will tell you that for years their black-legged sheep were known as "colley sheep," and the faithful dogs who tended them were "colley dogs."

The English people have a different answer. They say the word "colley" sprang from "coalie," the black soot off the kettle. And since the original Collies were black as soot, the name may have come from this old meaning.

But whatever the source, the Collie is known everywhere as the steadfast shepherd. In all weather he goes about his business: patrolling the sheep, rounding up the strays, guarding the flock. He will even fight his own relative, the wolf, to save the sheep. Not that he loves the sheep so much, but that he loves his master more.

The Merry Beagle

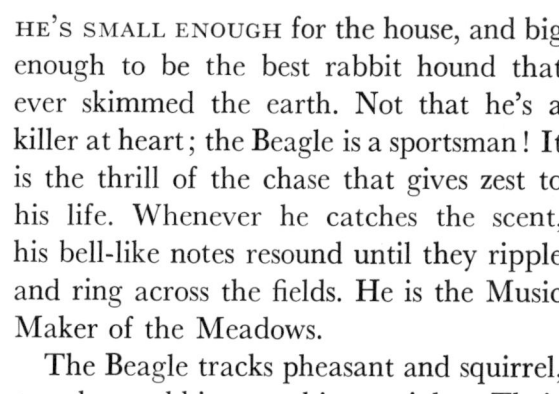

HE'S SMALL ENOUGH for the house, and big enough to be the best rabbit hound that ever skimmed the earth. Not that he's a killer at heart; the Beagle is a sportsman! It is the thrill of the chase that gives zest to his life. Whenever he catches the scent, his bell-like notes resound until they ripple and ring across the fields. He is the Music Maker of the Meadows.

The Beagle tracks pheasant and squirrel, too, but rabbits are his specialty. Their scent is very delicate, their ways cunning. Yet the Beagle can unravel the trickiest trails and make turnings and doublings as quick as any cottontail.

Back in the time of King Arthur this small, floppy-eared fellow was already a work hound, hunting hares for the King and his knights. Later, when Elizabeth I was Queen of England, she wanted to change the Beagle. She had him bred littler and littler until she could carry one around in a glove. The hunting squires of her day would fill their saddlebags with these miniature hounds, some only five inches high, and turn them loose on the heath to go a-hunting.

As working hounds they were a ridiculous failure! The Queen ruefully admitted her mistake, for the work of the Beagle became miniature, too, and his melodious baying smalled down to a piping squeak.

The "glove Beagle" went out of fashion in a hurry. Today's hound stands a full thirteen to fifteen inches. He's still a small-ish fellow compared to Setters and Pointers, but he's so well muscled that he looks big for his inches.

The name "Beagle" comes from the French *bégueule,* meaning a clamorous, baying creature. While the French named him, it was the English who made him popular. Beagling has long been one of their favorite sports, and we in America have adopted it.

What is beagling? Is it hiking to hounds? Of course it is. But so much more! Picture an autumn meadow, earth moist, breeze cool. Suddenly a cyclone of Beagles bursts onto the field. Noses busy, tails merry, long ears flying, they are puzzling out a rabbit trail. And panting in pursuit come the Whippers-In, men afoot in green coats with white stocks and breeches. One among them sights Molly Cottontail and lifts his voice—"Ho! Tally Ho!"

At the same instant the whole pack of Beagles catches the scent. In full cry they are on the line, circling the rabbit, pushing her hard, driving her ever onward. But by some miracle of trickery and timing she twists and turns, and slithers her way toward the meadow's end. There, in a tangle of brush, she dives into her hole.

Does it matter to hounds and men that Molly Cottontail has escaped? Not really. Most beaglers are secretly glad when she is driven safe into her hole to run another day.

It is the hard run, the swift pursuit, the thrilling matching of wits, and the constant interplay between hounds and men that make beagling such an exciting sport. And since beagling is done afoot, beaglers must be rugged, robust men to go the distance with their hounds.

But always there is a lone Beagle and a lone boy who were made for each other. They hunt or hike or swim together—sharing the good smells of woods and fields, in tune with all outdoors.

The Gentleman Boxer

RUDY DOCKY, a fast-tumbling clown from Austria, knows Boxers as well as he knows the sawdust ring. He believes that Boxers and circuses belong together. Using a balloon for a ball, Rudy has trained a whole troupe of Boxers to play a rip-roaring game of basketball. The game is such fun for dogs and audience alike that the act usually rates the center ring.

First, Rudy clumps into the spotlight, long shoes flapping like a beaver's tail. Under his arm he carries a bright balloon. (It is weighted with dried beans, so it won't float away.) Now he blows a shrill note on his whistle, and from the darkness of the wings ten Boxers come racing into the ring. They are wild to get their paws on the balloon.

As Rudy tosses it into the air, all ten players jump for it, and the game is on! Dancing on their hind legs, they butt and bat and shoot for the basket with heads, forepaws, and snub noses.

Time out! There's a foul. One fellow, hugging the ball tight, pricks it with his toenails. And *pffssst*—it bursts!

Quick, Rudy, a new ball!

Again the teams get set. Again the whistle. Again the game in full swing— players blocking, passing, dribbling, until the whole ring is churning with action. Rudy shouts advice to both teams: "Stick to him, Fritz! Don't double-dribble! Pass, Hans, pass!"

At last the tallest fellow shoots a basket, and with a two-point score his team has won. For the grand finale, all leftover balloons are tossed into the ring to be kicked and pricked for the sheer fun of it.

And so, with children shrilling in delight and dogs dancing in glee, the act is over.

"Boxers are born ball players," says Rudy Docky. "They use their paws the way a human fighter uses his fists. That," he explains, "is how they got their name."

The Boxer is a natural fighter—a lusty, gusty, hard-hitting fellow—but only when the need is clear. He seems to know when to fight and when not to. In his native Germany this level-headedness won him the title of Gentleman Boxer.

His ancestors were the mighty Mastiffs who grappled bears and boars, and held on grimly with teeth locked until the hunters arrived. These Mastiffs, crossed with Terrier strains, produced the Boxer we know today.

In appearance, the Boxer is a square sort of fellow, square of muzzle and square of stance. His coat, neat and tight, is of fawn color or brindle. In the days when he fought wild animals, it was necessary to dock his tail and crop his ears to keep them from being chewed. The custom still persists, even though today's Boxer never comes eye-to-eye with a bear.

The black mask is his trademark, with white accents for emphasis. The wrinkles between his eyes give him a sad and serious look that is quite misleading.

"Actually," Rudy says, "he is not sad at all. Quite the contrary, he is full of pranks. If the basketball game is not exciting enough, Fritz, the rascal, purposely punctures the balloon. But his best trick is to jump into the audience, upset the hot-dog vendor, and share the loot with his pals."

The Misunderstood Poodle

HE IS IN LOVE with life, but the most misunderstood dog on the earth. People think of him as a French fop. Yet he is neither French nor fop! He is probably German. "Pudel," meaning to splash about in the water, was his original name.

As for his foppishness, that is another mistaken idea. In spite of the ruff around his neck, the hair bracelets on his legs, and the bangles and bows in his pompadour, he is a vigorous fellow and highly intelligent.

Back in the sixteenth century the Poodle was a working dog in Germany, a waterfowl retriever. He loved to paddle in the water and would swim about for hours, even all night if necessary, to find a maimed duck.

His owners wanted to speed his swimming stroke, so they sheared the heavy wool from his hindquarters. He did swim faster as a result, but the men then began to worry about his health. Wouldn't shearing off his warm coat make him subject to pneumonia and rheumatism? Accordingly, they devised the Poodle cut—leaving the hair long on chest and ribs to protect the lungs, and leaving pompoms on the legs to protect the joints. The tuft on the tip of his tail became a signal flag, marking the dog's whereabouts as he swam through the water.

For two reasons the Poodle cut continues to be popular. First, at dog shows it is easier for judges to study bone structure if the body is not hidden by blankets of wool. The second reason is the thickness of his coat. A Poodle does not "shed out" as other dogs do; his wool keeps on growing and growing until it twists into wiry, ropelike curls. The messiness of such a coat, uncut, would be enough to change a gay, spirited dog into a frowsy rag rug. As it is, he comes home from his shearings bubbling with the joy of living.

Because of his intelligence, the Poodle is a star performer in the theater or circus. Whatever role he plays, he throws his whole heart into it. Acting is pie to him. At six months a Poodle pup is ready to follow his mother onstage as a tumbler. And before he is a year old, he can manage more serious roles.

You may have seen the talented Mam'selle Coco in the circus. In starched cap and apron, she pushes a carriage full of pups as deftly as any nursemaid. Or have you seen Mimi high-dive into a pool and then float around on a raft like some bathing beauty?

There is no limit to Poodle skills. They can turn somersaults both front and back, walk a tightrope, dance on rolling barrels, and the Great Pepi could even spell out words with children's blocks.

To suit every home, Poodles today come in three sizes—the big Standard, the midi-sized Miniature, and the tiny Toy. And to suit every fancy they come in a multitude of solid colors—black, white, *café au lait*, silver, gray, apricot, cream, blue, and brown. They are at home with clowns and elephants; or with huntsmen and their guns; or on Mamma's lap.

The French claim the Poodle as their own because of his *joie de vivre,* and have honored him as their national dog. They insist that Poodles are people, and they have a saying: *Un homme ferme est fidèle comme un caniche* (A steadfast person is as loyal as a Poodle).

18

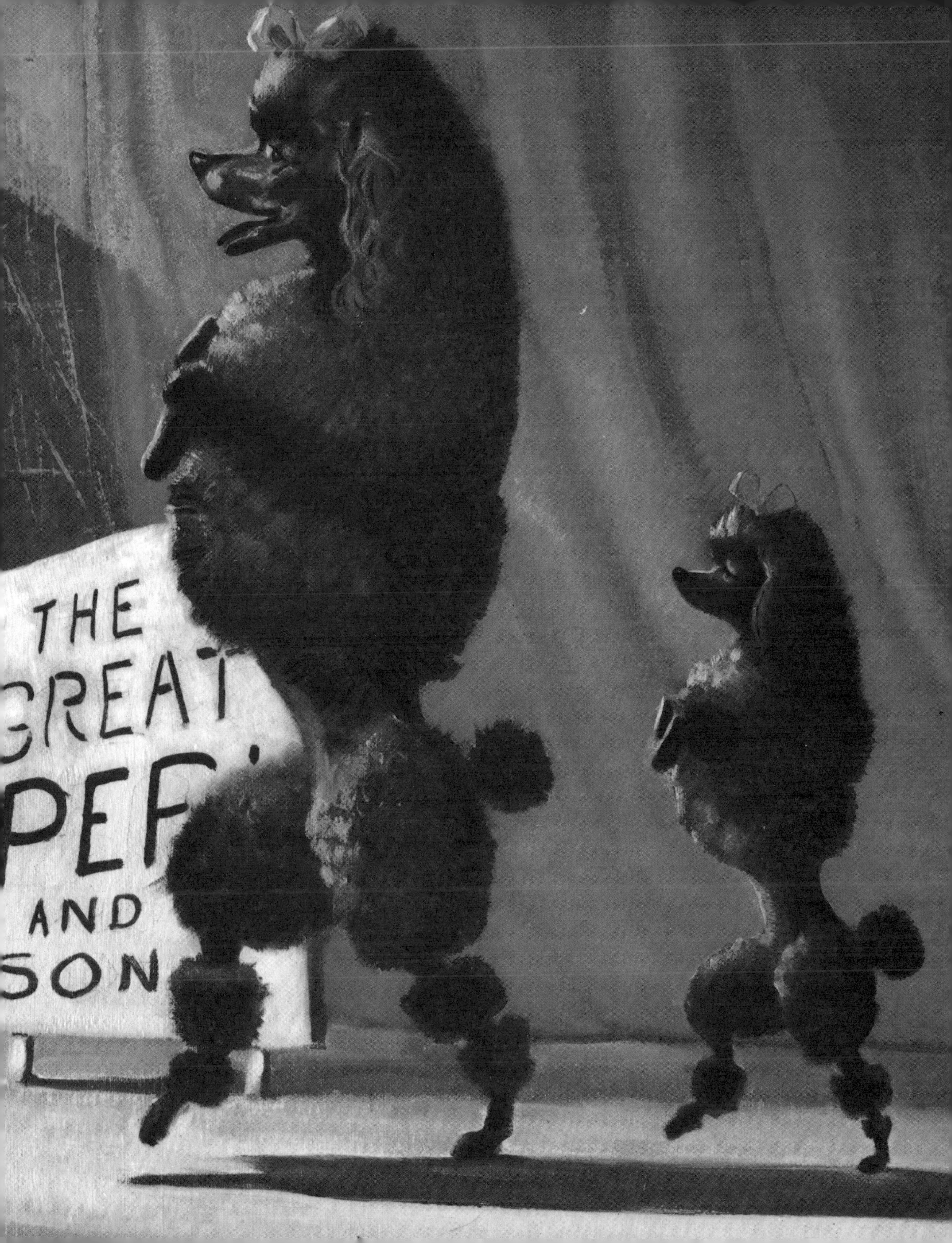
THE
AND
SON

Old Sour Mug, the Bulldog

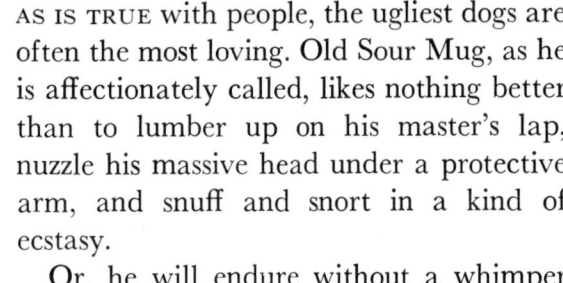

AS IS TRUE with people, the ugliest dogs are often the most loving. Old Sour Mug, as he is affectionately called, likes nothing better than to lumber up on his master's lap, nuzzle his massive head under a protective arm, and snuff and snort in a kind of ecstasy.

Or, he will endure without a whimper the tail-twistings and eye-pokings of a thoughtless child. He seems almost insensible to pain.

How can this be? Perhaps it is because once upon a time he was a bullfighter. For hundreds of years in old England, his ancestors provided a strange sport known as "Pinning the Bull." At a marketplace or some so-called garden, an arena was roped off. And within it a maddened bull was chained to a stake. The chain was long enough to give the bull plenty of freedom, but short enough to protect the spectators.

At the appointed hour the fight begins. Three eager dogs are tossed into the arena. By instinct they are drawn to the big beast. They shuffle forward, small moving shapes inching to death or victory.

For a moment the bull seems hypnotized. Then he slow-foots toward the dogs, head down, horns beginning to reach.

The nearest dog stops, braces himself. He sees the horns coming straight for him, dipping lower, slanting now for the hook. He feels the whuffing breath from the bull's red nostrils. He tries to swerve, as the other dogs rush in—but too late. The left horn catches him, rips his thigh, knocking him down in the dirt.

He is up at once, bleeding. The bull backs off for a return charge. Again the other dogs spring into the fray. But the bull clashes head on with the bleeding one. The time is now! With a quick upthrust of his jaw, the hurt dog clamps his teeth onto the bull's tender nose.

Plunging, pitching in pain, the huge beast jerks his head violently, shaking the dog like a rag; but he cannot shake free.

The crowd howls with joy at the dog's tenacity. "Stay with him! Hang on!"

The dog won't let go, even though the bull whirls him around, slaps him against the stake . . . again, and again. The pinning, pinching hold only tightens. Now the bull is dizzying. He can stand the pain no longer. As the crowd screams in frenzy, he sinks exhausted to earth.

For this savage sport a special breed, the Bulldog, was developed. He had to be broad of shoulder, but agile as a cat. His nose had to be flat and his nostrils uptilted so that he could breathe with his face up against a bull's. And his lower jaw had to be wide and undershot in order to grab and hold.

Sensational as bull-baiting was, it did not last. Men finally felt shame at matching a fifty-pound dog against half a ton of bull. Even though the dogs were not often killed, the suffering they endured was too cruel. And so, in 1835, the British banned the sport by law.

Dog lovers, however, did not let the Bulldog die out. They bred only the gentler ones until they developed the mildest, ugliest dog in the kingdom. He is still John Bull, the symbol of British tenacity, still the mascot of the British Navy. But his real place in the sun is as a child's pet—a wrinkled, endearing fellow with a toothy grin and a great, tender heart.

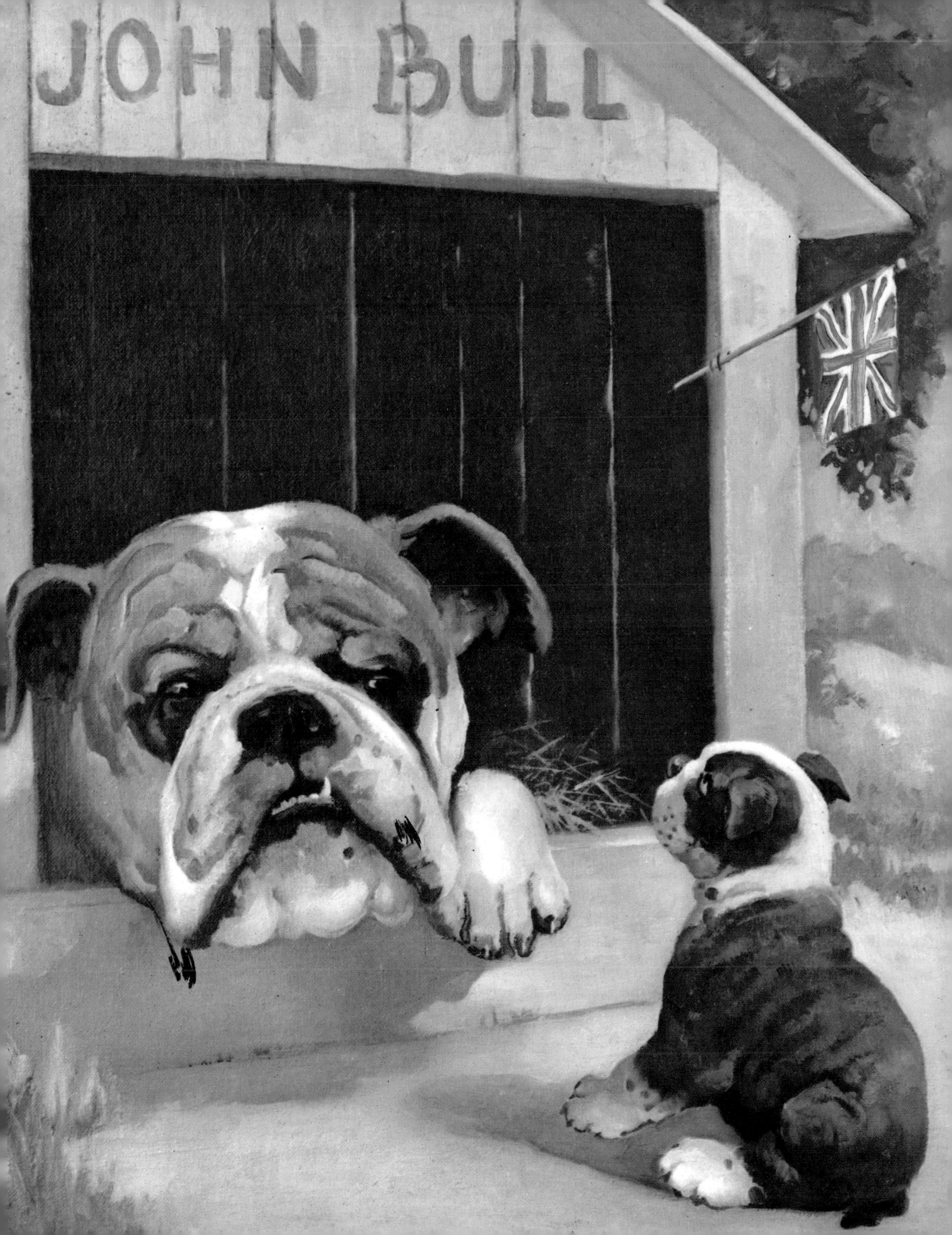
JOHN BULL

Pixie, the Cocker Spaniel

IN DAYS LONG AGO this littlest of the Spaniels was a bird dog. By instinct he was a hunter, and by training he became an expert at finding and flushing and retrieving.

In England, where woodcock abounded, he would thrash through brush and brier to rout a bird from its hideaway. Often he emerged scratched and bleeding, but his stump of a tail wagged importantly. He had flushed the woodcock into the air; the gun had downed it; and now he was delivering the prize into his master's hands. "Let's do it again!" his pleading eyes said.

And with the same eagerness he would plunge into the thicket again, unmindful of the cockleburs that latched onto his flopping, feathery ears.

Because this tireless hunter was such an expert on woodcock he earned the name "Cocking Spaniel." Of course, the "Spaniel" came from the country of his origin, which was Spain.

When the Cocker was introduced into America, a curious thing happened to him. He was taken out of the fields and into the bosom of the family. Over in England his pleasing appearance had been taken for granted. But Americans found him irresistible. They liked his silken coat and his handy size. But they were enchanted by his big, soulful eyes. He could look sad and glad all at the same time; though his face wore a melancholy expression, his tail was incessantly joyful.

Pixie, a wavy-coated red, was a typical house pet who never worked the fields at all. As a pup she had been full of mischief —chewing slippers, sneaking candies off the table, tipping over wastebaskets. But always she felt sorry afterward.

Knowing how sensitive she was, the family punished her just as they punished their own children—by banishing her to the Naughty Chair. It stood in a corner of the living room between soft, cushioned chairs; but it was uncomfortably stiff, with a hard scoop seat. After each offense Pixie was made to sit there for twenty minutes.

Of course, she detested the Naughty Chair. Sitting there made her feel so alone. Life went on all about her, the children romping and playing without so much as a look in her direction. As the minutes wore on, she became lonelier and lonelier until life was unbearable.

Never did a pup learn more quickly. Before she was a year old Pixie had outgrown her puppy tricks until the Naughty Chair was rarely used. Eventually she ignored it completely, sauntering by as if it did not exist.

But in the far recesses of her mind Pixie must have stored the memory. On the day when she came upon her own puppy chewing on a party slipper, she could not resist joining in the fun. Dancing around him in dizzy delight, she snatched the slipper away and gave it a fierce shake to show him just how it should be done. Then, heartily ashamed of herself, she leaped up onto the Naughty Chair to take the punishment for them both.

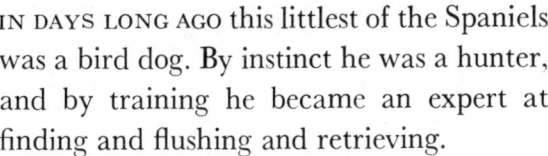
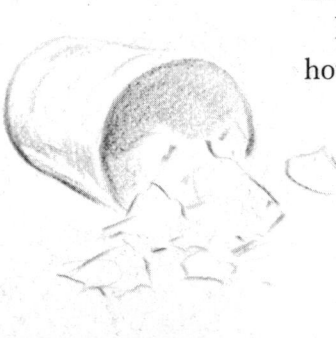

The German Shepherd

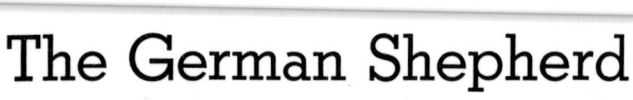
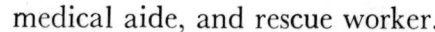

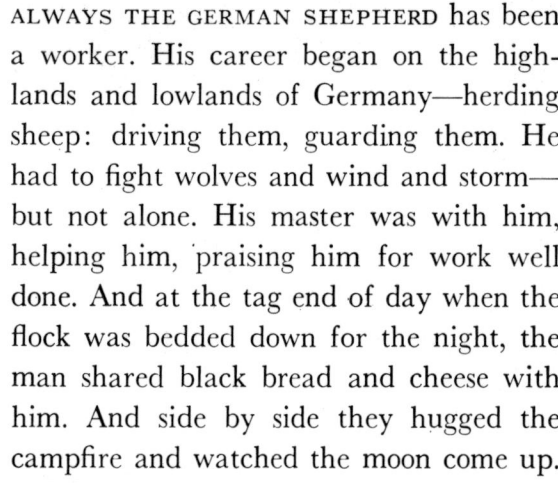

ALWAYS THE GERMAN SHEPHERD has been a worker. His career began on the highlands and lowlands of Germany—herding sheep: driving them, guarding them. He had to fight wolves and wind and storm—but not alone. His master was with him, helping him, praising him for work well done. And at the tag end of day when the flock was bedded down for the night, the man shared black bread and cheese with him. And side by side they hugged the campfire and watched the moon come up.

Life was good for the German Shepherd—the work and the sameness of his days and the sharing with his master.

Then Time changed the face of Germany. Steam trains came whistling across the land, carrying livestock to market; they made sheep-driving unnecessary. And settlers began pushing outward from the cities, shoving the flocks into the hinterlands. The big sheep ranges became smaller and smaller until they were all boxed in by fences. Now there was no need for protecting the sheep, and so no need for the shepherd dog!

The breed might have petered out if the German police had not foreseen a new role for the intelligent, clearheaded fellow. They trained him to attack criminals with the same ferocity he once attacked wolves. Soon the whole world knew of him not as a shepherd but as a police dog.

At the outbreak of World War I the police dog seemed ideally trained for combat services. The armies on all fronts began drafting him as scout, sentry, messenger, medical aide, and rescue worker.

But it remained for the blinded men left over from war to give new stature and new purpose to the police dog. Once again he became a good shepherd—leading, guiding, protecting.

Today thousands of German Shepherds are going to Seeing-Eye schools. They are bright and eager pupils. In a matter of months they learn to guide their masters through every sort of hazard. They signal down-steps by sitting; up-steps by stopping. More important, they develop a high capacity for reasoning. While *they* can walk under a scaffold or low awning, they swing clear of it for their blind companions.

To know one of these dog-graduates is to admire him to the point of hero-worship. His skills are almost human. Striding along at a calm, machinelike pace, he leads a blind person through the snarls of city traffic with no bumbling or hesitation.

The great miracle of the Shepherd's dedication is his aloofness toward temptation—tantalizing meat-and-gravy smells wafting out of restaurants, cats streaking in front of him or spitting in his face, even the come-play-with-me bark of some friendly mongrel. His long months of training, and his natural desire to serve and protect keep him on duty. In spite of distractions, he stays with his sightless master. Heads up, eyes forward, they go marching along together; a man-dog team held close—not by harness and handle but by love.

Once again the German Shepherd has found his work.

Pekingese, Little Lion

THE PEKINGESE is a paradox. He looks like a scrap of fluff, but lift him up and you find him surprisingly heavy. He is massive in front, like a lion, and sports a full, flowing mane. He is lion-hearted, too. I know of one, appropriately named King Richard, who defies even a Great Dane. Bringing out his prized toys, a tinkleball and a rubber bone, he takes a warlike stance beside them and roars in the giant's face.

Luckily the Great Dane always lopes off in disgust. This makes King Richard supremely happy. "See that?" his tail wags. "I am so fierce the big bully ran for his life."

But in many ways a Pekingese is more kitten than lion. He washes his whiskers and paws after eating, and he picks his way in and out among fine bric-a-brac as nimbly as a cat.

He is quite at home with fine things, for centuries ago his ancestors lived among porcelain and jade, teakwood and crystal. They were the palace dogs of China, the pampered pets of royalty, and they lived in great splendor and luxury.

The high priests held them in reverence because the great god Buddha was always depicted with a lion as his protector. And since there were no lions in China, the priests honored the "little lion." He became their Sacred Temple Dog.

Emperor T'ai Tsung used four lion dogs as escorts. Wherever he went, Peach Blossom and Bamboo Leaf strutted ahead, heralding his approach with short barks; Pomegranate and Precious followed in his wake, bearing the hem of the royal robe in their teeth.

Centuries later, the Empress Dowager Tzu Hsi composed a poem about the lion dog, and it reads almost like today's standard for the Pekingese.

Let the Lion Dog be small. Let him wear the mane of dignity around his neck; let him display the billowing tail over his back. Let his muzzle be black, and let it appear flat, as though sliced with a knife downward from the forehead.

Let his eyes be large and luminous. Let his ears be set like the sails of a war junk. Let his feet be tufted with plentiful hair so that his footfalls be noiseless.

For his color, let it be that of the true lion, a golden sable. Or the color of a red bear; or striped like a dragon, so that there may be dogs appropriate to every costume in the Imperial wardrobe.

The Empress also listed epicurean menus for the royal dogs:

Let his meat be the breast of quail, and the fins of sharks, and the liver of curlews. And let his drink be tea brewed from peach buds, or broth from the nests of sea swallows. And let all liquids be served in a throstle's eggshell.

For centuries the Sacred Temple Dogs thrived in the seclusion of the Imperial Court. Then in 1860, near the close of the Chinese War, British troops entered Peking and sacked the magnificent Summer Palace. In the deserted courtyard they found four little dogs wandering forlornly in a rose garden. To the English they were valuable pocket charms to be carried home as mementos. One they presented to Queen Victoria, and the other three were kept by fanciers of purebreds.

It was these royal refugees that established the new breed in the Western world. Today the Pekingese is lionized by all who admire courage and dignity in one so small.

The Coach Dog of Dalmatia

ONCE THERE WAS a black-spotted Dalmatian named Polka Dot. She belonged in equal measure to two boys *and* their two horses. Each summer the boys reluctantly went off with their family to live in England. Polka Dot was left behind in a boarding kennel.

But one year the family could not bring themselves to leave her at the kennel because she was about to give birth to her first litter. They wanted her to be in surroundings as nearly like her accustomed ones as possible. The foster home should include kind parents, of course, and two children at least, and there *had* to be horses! For Polka Dot was a true Dalmatian, a coach dog who liked horses the way a bee likes flowers.

Polka Dot's new home turned out to be exactly to her liking. Wesley Dennis, the horse artist, was chosen to care for her, not only because he was a dog's kind of man, but because he had two boys and six horses!

Polka Dot found complete happiness with her new family. She soon gave birth to her puppies—eight chubby ones—in an apple box in Wesley's studio. To his shock, but not to hers, they were all-white, with no indication of the black spots to come!

The summer days lazied themselves away. Between nursings, Polka Dot nosed around in the stable and accompanied the horses on short gallops. She brought up her puppies to like horses, too.

Then one day came word from England:

We are bringing home a world champion Dalmatian to be mated with Polka Dot. At weaning time please give her puppies away.

Sorrowfully Wesley called his best friends and gave them their choice of the roly-poly youngsters until only one was left. Quite suddenly he realized how empty his studio would seem without a pup tearing his paint rags or nipping at his toes. "I'll keep the last one myself!" he decided. "And I'll name him Dice."

And so, when Polka Dot went back home, little Dice was left as a keepsake.

By show standards Dice would never win "Best of Breed." He was handsome and well sprinkled with dense black spots, but some of them ran together, a fault by show standards. "He wouldn't like dog shows anyway," said Wesley. "He would prefer horse shows. Horses are his life!"

It was true. The big thing in Dice's day was his morning canter with Wesley and his mount. He was so fearful that some day Wesley would go off without him that right after breakfast he stood watch by the riding boots. If for some reason Wes was delayed, Dice went to sleep on top of them!

"Riding with Dice is fun," Wesley said. "He never gets under my horse's feet, or runs ahead and chases sheep, as my other dogs did. He paces himself to my horse and travels alongside, happy as a gypsy.

"If it can be avoided, Dice and I are never separated. When I went to the Grand Canyon on the Brighty story, I missed him so much I sent him bones by parcel post."

One thing strange about Dice was that he couldn't bear getting wet. It was funny to see him try to cross a brook without wetting his feet. Caught in the rain, he would try to run under the drops. In eight years he had only two baths. He suffered so much from the scrubbings that Wesley just gave them up.

"Who needs a bath?" he would say to Dice. "You always look clean, though I can't say you're spotless!"

Fox Terrier–Happy-Go-Lucky

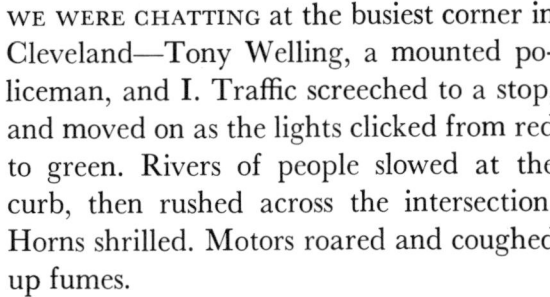

WE WERE CHATTING at the busiest corner in Cleveland—Tony Welling, a mounted policeman, and I. Traffic screeched to a stop, and moved on as the lights clicked from red to green. Rivers of people slowed at the curb, then rushed across the intersection. Horns shrilled. Motors roared and coughed up fumes.

Yet in all the noise and bustle a private little drama was taking place. A black and white Fox Terrier was dancing on his hind feet so that he could touch noses with the obviously delighted police horse. The two creatures were of one world and one mind, and for them this other world of noise and smell did not exist.

"What do you suppose they are saying?" I asked Tony Welling, for both horse and dog were making whuffing, snorting noises.

"At first I couldn't tell, either," he admitted. "But now I understand."

"You understand what?"

"What Pepper says and what my Morgan answers."

The policeman cocked his finger at a driver who ran the yellow light. He had one eye on traffic, one on the little scene before us. "Each day is different," he said. "Sometimes it's just jabber, and sometimes it's important. But you . . ." he blushed in embarrassment, "you wouldn't understand, even if I told you."

"Oh yes, I would."

"All right. But if you doubt me, or laugh, I won't go on."

"I promise." And that was the last sound I uttered until he finished.

"Pepper is a city dog," Tony Welling began. "Yes, I know lots of Fox Terriers are city dogs. But Pepper is a downtown dog.

It's like living in a canyon, the way he lives —a canyon of stone buildings. Not a tree in sight, not even a bush or blade of grass. Plenty of fireplugs and concrete sidewalks, but no trees!

"My horse, Skip, is his only link with the green world outside. When Skip talks, his breath is sweet-smelling with hay and clover. And what he says is full of danger, excitement, and adventure. Why, the day after the circus fire, when Skip rescued nineteen horses from a burning tent, he told Pepper all about it.

"How do I know? Well, first Pepper snuffed at Skip's burned whiskers and forelock and said, 'Hmmm, what's this strange smell I smell?'

"And then I swear Skip told him the whole story. Else why did the dog begin to lick the burned places on Skip's neck, and why did he whine and whimper and make over him exactly like he was a hero? Which he was!"

Tony Welling stopped to scold a jaywalker before going on. "Pepper must somehow sense that Skip is a link to his past. Over in England, you know, Fox Terriers traveled with horses and hounds, tracking the fox to his den and then digging him out of it. That's why they were bred.

"But Pepper? Chances are he'll never see a fox! Mice is the best he can do. Like as not he'll live out his days in that swell hotel over yonder—with no trees, no grass, not even a shrub."

The policeman sighed. "But look at him. He's happy, living part of his life by proxy, the way some folks live through the books they read. It's just lucky for him that he found Skip, a horse that can talk!"

The Pointing Dogs

WHEN THE FIRST haze of Indian summer hangs over the woodlands, a feeling of wanderlust stirs the blood of Pointers and Setters. If their masters do not come for them, they pace restlessly up and down their kennel runs, and at night their sleep is broken, and they yammer in their dreams. But their masters nearly always do come, for they, too, are stirred by the same urgency.

All dogs have the hunting instinct. In some it reaches a transcendency. With the big-ranging Pointer the feeling is so strong that, if it should be denied, he will break free of his wire pen and hunt on his own. So great is his need.

How well and how simply he is named! *La punta,* in Spanish "the point." Only a few historians are convinced that the Pointer originated in Spain, but all describe his forebears as slow-going, heavy-footed "potterers" with irritable dispositions. English fanciers bred him to their foxhounds and as a result he worked faster and surer. Later they crossed his blood with Setter blood, and then his temper sweetened.

One Englishman, Sam Price by name, bent all his efforts to create a Pointer with a nose so quick and sensitive that he would have to gallop across the fields in order to keep up with it! Price was also credited with introducing Greyhound strains for getaway speed. In time he produced a World Champion Pointer named Bang.

Bang had everything. Nose, speed, joy of working. He quartered a field like a zigzag of lightning. And when he came upon his birds, he froze in his tracks, hypnotized by the scent. His tail went rigid and his whole body pointed as if a tight thread were stretched from unerring nose to birds.

When Bang's son, Bang-Bang, arrived in America, he set the style for a dog who loved to hunt even better than he loved his master!

The Pointer is not the only breed that has learned the art of pointing. There are three Setters—the English, the Irish, and the Scotch—who also point their game. They all have the same heritage, and the same desire to hunt. Yet how different they are in appearance and character!

Strangely, it is the long-haired English Setter and the sleek-coated Pointer who are most alike. Both are white-bodied and freckled—some with black spots, some with liver or chestnut, some with orange or lemon. When they are on point, their white coats stand out sharply against the russet tones of autumn.

And they are both intensely competitive in spirit. In Field Trials each one is determined to find birds faster than the dog he is matched against. Even their puppies entered in "Nursery Stakes" show that same competitive spirit. Of course they are scatterbrained sometimes, and chase dragonflies or sparrows instead of game birds, but all is forgiven in the Nursery Stakes.

What of the Irish Red Setter and the Scotch Black-and-Tan Gordon? How good are they in the field? In all honesty, they seldom win at the big trials. Perhaps one

English Setter (above)

The Pointer

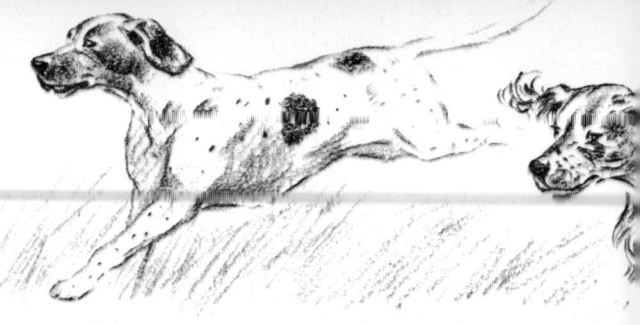

day they will step out and challenge their English cousins, but meanwhile they are more petted at home than praised afield.

The striking beauty of the Irish Setter has almost been his undoing as a hunter. His flaming mahogany coat became such a temptation to show-dog people that they kept breeding for heightened color, instead of bird sense. But they could not breed out the hunting instinct entirely, and the National Red Setter Club has been restoring the dog to higher performance standards. Still, many an owner is quite willing to leave his loving Irishman at home, for when the landscape is all red and gold with autumn, the dog is scarcely visible to the hunter.

IRISH

The Black-and-Tan Gordon is also color-handicapped. He is a sturdy, dependable worker, but he too blends with the land-scape, especially at dusk when hunting is at its best. Then his color melts into burned-over tree stumps and earthy browns. Even if he pointed hour on end, he might go un-seen.

All three Setters are descended from the famed "Setting Spaniels" who long ago crouched, or *set,* as they neared their birds. The fowler would then throw a huge net over birds and dogs both, and so gather them in.

But with the invention of firearms the net

SCOTCH

was discarded, and the dogs were taught to stand and point game instead of to set.

There is a magnificent and praiseworthy restraint in the pointing dog. His instinct is to snatch his game. But with training he will hunt his heart out, and when he finds the birds, his whole body will stiffen into a direction flag. Rightfully, the birds are his. If he were a child he might scream: "They're mine! Mine! Let me at 'em!" Instead, he suppresses his own desire and gives the glory to his master.

Of all the pointing breeds, the Pointer is generally conceded to be the best bird finder. Why, then, does *anyone* choose a Setter?

One reason may well be that the Setter loves the master for himself, while the Pointer likes any man with a gun! Then, too, not every hunter can keep up with such a fast, wide-ranging fellow. Some prefer a dog who works in close and looks often to the master for help and direction.

The bold, far-roving Pointer is fine if the hunter seeks a big bag of birds, but if he prefers a close-quartering dog and unflag-ging devotion, then a Setter is the happy answer.

So there you have them—the long-haired English, Irish, and Scotch Setters, and the short-haired Pointer. Good, honest game dogs all, and yours for the choosing.

ENGLISH

34

Gordon Setter (above)

Irish Setter

Speaking as a Springer

DEAR READER: *I'd like to set paw to paper and do my own chapter in my own way. I am a Springer Spaniel, white with black tickings. Tickings are little splashes of color, like freckles.*

"Baldwin of Lockridge" is my kennel name. But The Gunner (he's my boss) calls me "Boy." He calls me other things, too. Whenever he asks me to teach a young pup how to spring a rabbit or flush a bird, then he calls me "The Professor." I'd rather not be the professor. Please don't misunderstand. I like puppies. But they puzzle me! When the air is delicious with the smell of pheasant, how can they possibly stalk a butterfly? How can they do it?

Me? I just live to hunt! Give me a crisp autumn day, with The Gunner at my heels, and I'm in my glory. There's one hunt I'll never forget. It was the time when I took command.

The Gunner puts me down in a cornfield, in a world of teasing, tickling smells. "Spring 'em out, Boy!" he says. Well, hardly had I sampled the wind before I'd found bird scent. With a rush I followed that scent, my tail beckoning The Gunner to come along.

Everything happened fast. The birds were there all right—a veritable nide of pheasant. I sailed into them, and as they exploded into the air, I heard the gun crack twice. All except one cock kept on going. He began spinning and tumbling earthward. And then he did a strange thing. Suddenly he wheeled back toward the cornfield, where he swooped in for a landing.

I marked the spot and raced toward it, but when I got there I saw nothing but the dust he was raising. What a runner he was! Only the tip of his wing had been hit and he was running like wind, diving down the corn rows, doubling back again. His scent was strong and I sprinted after it, twisting and turning until I was dizzy.

In the distance I could hear The Gunner calling me in with deep disgust in his voice. But I couldn't stop now! The bird was trying to trick me. I had to outwit him! I circled far around, and when he darted into thick cover, I jumped him and grabbed his plump body in my mouth. In triumph I carried him back to The Gunner.

Well, you should've heard the boss! He laughed and laughed, but the pride in his voice made me wag from stem to stern. "Boy," he said huskily, "you've got character! You had to be disobedient to me, or to your job, and you made the right choice. If every man had a dog like you, fewer birds would be wasted. You're a conservationist, that's what you are!"

This story makes me out a hero, but honestly I have my limitations. First, I don't point game birds like a Pointer or Setter; I rush in and spring them. I'm a Springer Spaniel, you know.

Second, I am not as great a retriever in rough, icy waters as, say, the Labrador. I just haven't the size or coat for it.

When I meet a Pointer or a Retriever in the field, I go right up to him, give his nose a poke and a sniff, and say, "All right! Suppose you can do your particular job better than I. I'm an all-around bird dog. I find. I flush. I retrieve. I can give The Gunner as much good hunting as three specialists! That's me, fellow, a lot of dog in one."

Yours for good hunting,
BALDWIN OF LOCKRIDGE

P.S. There is one thing I seldom do, and that is be a watchdog. I hate being suspicious of everyone and barking all day. Well, I just like people—that's all.

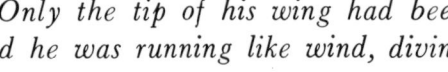

The Labrador, King of Retrievers

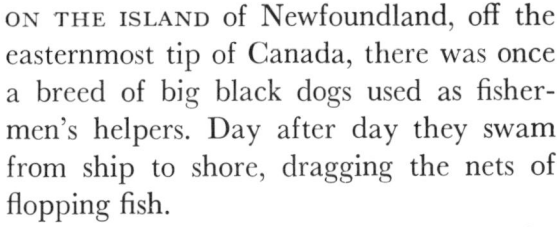

ON THE ISLAND of Newfoundland, off the easternmost tip of Canada, there was once a breed of big black dogs used as fishermen's helpers. Day after day they swam from ship to shore, dragging the nets of flopping fish.

For years they had been known as St. John's Water Dogs, after the Bay of St. John, where they worked. But in 1830 an Englishman, the Earl of Malmesbury, renamed them. At Poole Harbor, near his home, he liked to watch the ships from Canada unload their catch. What fascinated him was not the cargo of white-bellied fish; it was the sailors' sleek-haired dogs! He learned that they would retrieve fish or fowl in any water, in any weather.

The Earl was envious. His own Spaniels were expert at flushing a bird into the air, but when it fell into choppy waters, they were handicapped by their long coats in swimming after it. He needed a bold, short-haired dog to fetch the bird.

One day he bargained with a ship's captain and bought several of the coal-black dogs. The Earl's sense of geography being somewhat hazy, he called them Labrador Retrievers instead of Newfoundland Retrievers.

The Englishman never ceased to marvel at his new water dogs. He wrote to a friend, "My Labradors have so close a coat it turns the water off like oil. And, most uncommon, they have a tail like an otter's, short and thick, which makes an excellent rudder in swimming."

To sportsmen, however, the real miracle of today's Labrador is his self-control. A duck can whirr right past his nose, and he will remain steady. Even when the gun barks and the duck tumbles out of the sky, he neither flinches nor pursues. He waits for the command, "Fetch!" Then he's off like a bullet, leaping ten feet into the water, heading for the spot where the bird fell. On calm days he brings it back with lightning speed. But when wind and tide are high, the fallen bird is often carried out of his sight. Howling for help, he looks ashore, his raised head asking, "Where, Boss? Where?"

The boss answers with his arm. "Way to the right!" he waves. "Out farther. Farther!" To signal after signal the dog responds. When at last he finds his bird, he lifts it with tender mouth, and swims all the way back to his master.

"For me," one hunter says, "this beautiful teamwork between us is the thrill of the sport."

Another hunter, a white-haired veteran, claims that his thrill comes when the bird is delivered so gingerly that not a feather is ruffled. "What other animal," he asks, "would offer such a tasty morsel to me instead of devouring it himself?"

Most Labradors are naturally soft-mouthed. The same old hunter tells this remarkable story. His frolicsome pup Satin-Soot was at play one day with his litter sister. Bounding in and out of a creek, she was chasing Satin-Soot, who was carrying something in his mouth.

Curious, the old man called the puppy in and took from between his sharp teeth a live baby thrush, whole and unhurt! With lavish praise, he made this incident the puppy's first lesson in retrieving.

Boston Terrier–All American

IN THE YEAR 1870 a coal stoker boarding his ship in Liverpool fastened his woolen pea jacket tighter about his body. The captain eyed him suspiciously, for the day was sultry and the man needed a coat no more than a dog needs two tails. The truth was that under the jacket the stoker had a dog which he planned to hide down in the engine room and carry to America.

This was no ordinary household pet; he was a prize bull-and-terrier professional fighter. The stoker knew that his dog would bring ready money in Boston; he had sold similar ones in the city before. But he never dreamed that this particular dark-brindled chap would turn out to be the founding sire of a new American breed.

When the ship docked, the day was cool and the dog was smuggled off successfully. A Mr. Hooper bought the stowaway, but not because he wanted a fighting dog. He liked the dapper look of him—the snow-white bib, the white muzzle that blazed up over his head, the perky ears, and the impish twinkle in his eye. Here, he thought, was a fellow with character. It would be a fine thing to have pups in his image!

He called the dog Judge and mated him with an all-white Terrier. To Mr. Hooper's delight the pups were not only brindle in color, but were carbon copies of their sire.

In time, dog fanciers bought up Judge's pups and his grandpups, too, and deliberately created the Boston Terrier. The violence of the fighter was completely bred out, and gentleness bred in.

Judge Tobias, whose lineage went all the way back to Hooper's Judge, was one Boston Terrier I knew well. I can still see Toby gazing up at me, one ear pricked, one flopped over.

Toby was all things to all people. With children he was a boisterous playfellow, retrieving balls and sticks until he wore them out. To prowlers he was a growling threat.

But with Grandmother, a fragile little lady, he was gentleness itself. When she fell one day and fainted from the pain of a broken hip, he licked her face until she came back to consciousness. Then he ran for help.

While she was in the hospital, well-meaning friends and family said, "Toby is too frisky for an invalid on crutches. He should be given to some relative, or a neighbor."

But Grandmother was horrified. Who would bake his favorite bran muffins? Who would make his ragdoll toys? Of course, Toby stayed. And never once did he dive between her crutches, or even brush against them. Instead, he hovered about her like some diminutive nurse, softly murmuring encouragement as she hobbled from room to room.

The only time he left her side was when the ladies of the sewing circle met at his house. The click of shears filled his soul with terror, reminding him no doubt of the day his ears were cropped.

On sewing days Toby slunk off and fished the afternoon away at his own private pond. Sometimes a bluegill leaped right at him, surprising him nearly out of his wits. The big ones got away, but there was always a little one he caught and fetched home. Then when the sewing ladies were gone, Grandmother rolled it in crumbs and fried it for his supper.

In cozy little ways like this Toby gave Grandmother good reason to live on for a long, long time.

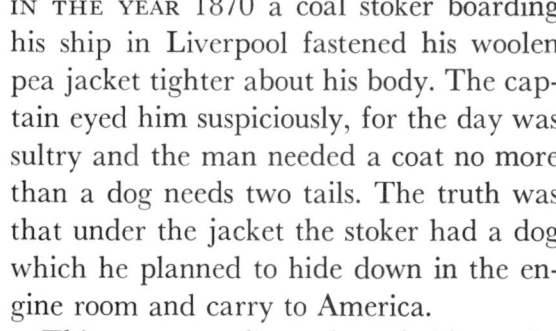

TO THE POND

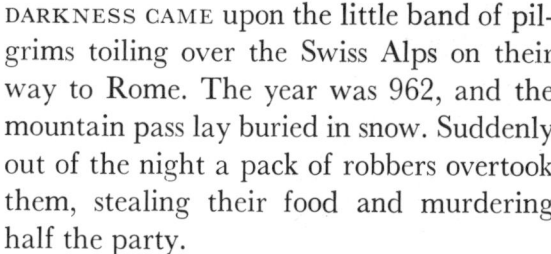

The Saint Bernard, Dog of Mercy

DARKNESS CAME upon the little band of pilgrims toiling over the Swiss Alps on their way to Rome. The year was 962, and the mountain pass lay buried in snow. Suddenly out of the night a pack of robbers overtook them, stealing their food and murdering half the party.

The survivors roped themselves together and made their slow way down the mountain to the valley of Aosta in Italy. Here Brother Bernard, a monk, listened to their tale of horror. He was a silent man, but when aroused he had the strength of an avalanche. Next day he stormed up the mountain with only a handful of men. And when he came upon the killers, his quiet rage awed them; they fled in fright.

This tragedy at the pass fired Brother Bernard with a plan. At the very site of the massacre he would build a hospice where travelers could find refuge from bandits and blizzards.

Over the years he raised enough money to build a monastery. It was bleak on the outside, but warm and friendly within. Here, pilgrims and peddlers, and migrant workers found comfort and safety.

News of the sanctuary spread. More and more people braved the pass. But some never reached the hospice; they lost their way, or were buried in avalanches of snow.

The monks were troubled. What good was their shelter if many travelers never reached it? What more could be done?

Were dogs the answer? Could the native Swiss hounds be of help? They were descendants of the huge Molossus dogs of Asia, and renowned for their scenting powers. The monks knocked on cottage doors in the valleys, asking: "Would you give one of your dogs to help in the rescue of lost wayfarers?"

Some farmers agreed. And from these Alpine hounds the monks developed a staunch breed of dogs, so keen of scent they could track human footprints days old; and if the trail ended in a snowslide, they would paw into the deepest drifts to find the lost traveler beneath.

Through the centuries these Saint Bernard dogs saved 2,500 lives. History pictures them with a cask of wine, and food strapped to a harness. Actually their rescue methods were even more dramatic. When a half-frozen victim was found, two of the dogs would lie down, one on either side, to warm him. A third licked his face to revive him, and a fourth ran back to the monks, his deep voice baying for help.

The heroic dog Barry saved forty victims of snow sleep. One was a little girl, whom he revived and then coaxed to ride on his back to the shelter. Ever since his death in 1814 the monks have never been without a dog named Barry. And on an escarpment overlooking the hospice they have placed a life-size statue of the original Barry.

Today, with telephone lines, and highways over the Alps, and railroads tunneling through them, the rescue dogs have less work to do. But in a shelter high in the Himalayas of Tibet, the Saint Bernard's aid to travelers is still of prime importance.

In the United States the big, handsome fellow is often found in country homes, where there is room enough for a giant dog. He romps with the children in oversized happiness, and he licks away their tears when they are hurt. By instinct he is always the comforter.

Mustard Seed, the Pomeranian

IT IS MIRACULOUS how important a dog can become in the life of a person suddenly deprived of freedom. In a Chicago suburb a teen-age girl, Bobby Ann, was stricken by polio. Before her illness, horses were her life. She hacked across country for fun; she showed her horse in jumping classes, and had a wall of blue ribbons to prove it. Just when life seemed as full of promise as a sunrise, the illness hit. After the fever died down, she was helpless, except for one arm.

Now a plucky new Bobby Ann emerged. Of course she had been game when she took the high hurdles on her Thoroughbred. But then it was the horse that had the look of eagles. Now Bobby Ann had the look in her own eyes.

Her first thought was: "I'd love to paint! I never had time before." So she asked for paints and canvas, and began to work with watercolors and oils. But even with her new hobby, there were lonely days. To herself she wondered about a dog. Surely there must be a tiny one, easy to lift and hold in one arm.

Hopefully, she sent for books on dogs. Skipping over the big dogs, she turned to the toy breeds; and suddenly, looking out at her from a color photograph, she saw the foxy face of a Pomeranian. She was captivated! In great excitement she scanned the description. One line said all she needed to know: *Usually under six pounds, some as little as three.*

Gleefully, Bobby Ann closed the book. Her search was over.

The dog, an orange-sable Pomeranian, arrived on her birthday with his kennel name, "Mustard Seed," printed in big letters on his crate. "I'll keep that name!" she said as she hugged the ball of fluff close.

"The color is right," her parents agreed.

"Ho-ho!" Bobby Ann's young brother burst out laughing. "You gonna call him Mussy for short? Or Seedy? Ho-ho-ho!"

Bobby Ann smiled, then sobered. She glanced from face to face. "Do you remember when I was sick?"

The room grew very quiet as she went on. "One day when the minister came to call, he said, 'If you have faith no bigger than a mustard seed, nothing shall be impossible to you.'" The little Pom nudged her to keep on scratching his ear. "And now nothing shall!"

Mustard Seed served his purpose well. He learned to carry messages to and fro, from bedroom to kitchen. And each day he brought his comb to Bobby Ann to have his coat groomed.

To entertain visitors, Bobby Ann taught him to pirouette like a ballerina, and roll over, and jump through a hoop. She wanted to prove to her friends that her world was a normal, lively place. Guests now left reluctantly, almost in envy, not conscious at all of Bobby Ann's limitations.

As for Mustard Seed, he strutted big to make up for his littleness. Indeed, he had a heritage to justify his pride. Bobby Ann painted a picture of his ancestors—the great sledge dog of the Arctic and the Wolf-Spitz, who drove cattle in Germany. It was in Germany, in Pomerania, that fanciers bred the Spitz down to toy size.

But all through the years of evolution, the toy Pom has kept his resemblance to the big dogs of the Arctic. You can see it in the thickness of his coat, in the plumed tail over his back, in the wise look on his foxlike face. He is still the majestic dog of the North—in miniature!

The Great Dane

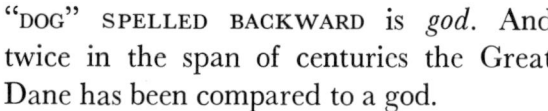

"DOG" SPELLED BACKWARD is *god*. And twice in the span of centuries the Great Dane has been compared to a god.

In early Greece he was likened to Apollo. In spite of his colossal size, he moved with all the grace of the mythological Greek god of poetry and music.

In Roman times he was called Vulcan, for the god of fire. He earned the title because of his deep store of courage. Tossed into an arena of wild lions, he fought like an unquenchable flame. The lion outweighed him three to one, and he wore natural armor. His mane was a shield, protecting neck and throat. And he carried savage weapons: his forelegs were clubs, his claws curved swords, his teeth stilettos. Yet often he lost the battle to the lean, short-haired dog. Spectators who had wagered on the lion lost miserably, but they would cheer the winner, shouting, "He is not dog! He is Vulcan!"

This fighting prowess won for the Great Dane a continuing place in history. In seventeenth-century Germany he was used to hunt wild boars. Again the contest was uneven; a hound's tooth is no match for a foot-long tusk that can rake and gore. One German Duke owned a pack of 600 boar hounds; they practically wiped out the ferocious beast in his duchy. Next they tackled bear and wolf, until at length the Black Forest was pronounced safe—even for Little Red Riding Hood!

The Germans developed three types of boar hounds: the brindle, the solid-colored (fawn, black, or blue), and the *Tiger Hunds,* which were white with black splotches.

"Great Dane" is a curious misnomer. Of course the dog *is* great in size and courage, but he is in no sense Danish. As it happened, several boar hounds were shipped to Denmark and their puppies later sent to France, where the French promptly labeled them *Grand Danois,* meaning "Great Dane." The spotted *Tiger Hund* they renamed "Harlequin." Both these French terms have prevailed.

In America the Great Dane was banned from shows for a long time because he stirred up fights with other dogs. That set the handlers to squabbling, and then the owners, until there was no end to the fracas. However, breeders had faith in the huge dogs. In a long-term program they improved his temper until he became as tractable as a big dog could be. But it was years before the American Kennel Club accepted him.

Meanwhile, more and more people fell in love with the beauty and magnificence of the Great Dane. And he was so adaptable! He could be hitched to a child's sleigh in winter or a pony cart in summer. Horsemen liked him, too, because he could stay the distance with a good horse all day.

The Great Dane has his own sense of fun. To him small dogs and cats are fun. He gently rolls them over like tumbleweeds and bunts them with his big nose. One owner says of her Dane, "My King Haakon is a regal fellow who scorns ordinary toys; but our cat is essential to him. When I laugh at his love for plain little Tillie, he silences me with a glance that says: 'Is this so unthinkable? Even gods and kings have pets, you know.'"

Chihuahua—Midget of Mexico

OF ALL DOGS in the world, the Chihuahua (Che-WAH-wah) is the smallest. He is so tiny he can be tucked into a man's pocket or a lady's muff, and still leave room for a pair of gloves!

As a puppy he is no bigger than a mouse. Full grown, he weighs a mere two or three pounds. In the show ring—if his conformation is good—the less he weighs the greater his chances of winning.

He was not always this small. His forebears were twelve-to-fifteen-pound dogs that roamed wild in the hinterlands of Mexico. Food was scarce in the barren hills, and life perilous. Like the wild mustang, the Chihuahua diminished in size over the centuries, but he never lost his alert, "I'm-ready-for-anything" attitude.

Today's model Chihuahua should have good bone, and be straight of legs, front and back. His skull should be rounded as an apple. His ears should be big and flaring outward. He can be any color. However, his eyes and nose must match—whether they are brown or black, fawn or red, or even blue! And his tail should be carried in a loop. Owners say, "When he wags in happiness, he hoops!"

Surprisingly, the Chihuahua's sense of smell is not very keen, but his vision is remarkably sharp. His eye focuses much like the human eye. Instead of recognizing his master by form and then by smell, as other dogs do, he identifies him quickly by sight.

This tiny creature is a canine snob. He is not interested in mingling with other breeds; in reality he prefers people.

"Nothing pleases a Chihuahua more than to cuddle close beside you..." These are the words of Madame Patti, the great opera star, who was as petite in her way as her Chihuahua in his.

Her meadowlark voice gave so much joy to people everywhere that they lavished gifts upon her. Kings presented her with diamonds and rubies. Peasants brought new-baked bread and grapes to her dressing-room door. But of all gifts, the midget of Mexico was her favorite. And this was the way of it.

At the close of a farewell concert in Mexico City, while Madame Patti was still bowing and the audience still shouting their Bravos, a man bearing a large bouquet ran down the aisle to the stage. The little diva reached for the flowers and impulsively buried her nose in them. To her stunned amazement, up popped a saucy head, ears pricked, eyes quizzical. There in the bright circle of light the two diminutive creatures studied each other.

A sudden hush fell over the opera house as Madame Patti lifted the Chihuahua out from the bouquet and began to speak. "Dear friends!" she said almost in a whisper. "From each country I like to take with me a token of remembrance, but never before have I received a memento so dear."

She held aloft the wee creature with the wingspread ears. "In your country," she said, "butterfly becomes the beautiful word *farfalla,* and for his magnificent ears I shall call him that all the days of his life."

The orchestra began playing the Mexican national anthem. Enraptured, the audience sang along with Madame Patti. Their own native dog from the State of Chihuahua would be traveling all around the world with the little diva whom they adored. Their joy in giving was complete.

Herr Dobermann's Pinscher

ABOUT A HUNDRED years ago, in the city of Apolda, Germany, there lived a man who truly loved dogs. His name was Herr Louis Dobermann, and it was his dream to create a new and very specialized breed.

"I know I can do it!" he told his best friend, the bell ringer of Apolda.

The man shrugged and repeated the question. "Why not? You are Herr Louis, the town's dogcatcher! You have all manner of dogs to work with."

He did indeed, but that made his task of selection all the harder. What he really had in mind was to produce a "sharp" dog, and by "sharp" he meant one that would attack as quickly as a struck match bursts into flame. His city was rich in factories and foundries and fine homes, and the owners were continually asking Herr Louis for good watchdogs.

And so he began to plan a scientific breeding program. For his perfect watchdog he needed the grace, swiftness, and leaping ability which Terriers could provide. And he needed the quick mind of the old-time German Shepherd, and the keen nose of the Pointer, and the good shoulders and quarters of the big cattle-dogs of Germany. But could all these traits be blended?

As luck would have it, Herr Louis had recently picked up one of the lively Terriers known as Pinschers. She was little and quick, and lithe as a deer. He mused to himself: "If little Schnuppe were bred to a bigger dog, her offspring might well be taller Pinschers—not clumsy at all, but lithe as she."

Herr Dobermann's dream did not come true in a year or even two. Although Schnuppe occasionally produced a miniature throwback, she did become the matriarch of the new breed. After several dog-generations of careful mating, her great-great-grandchildren became the big Doberman Pinschers we know today.

In appearance the Doberman is most distinctive and distinguished. He is the lean aristocrat of dogdom—tall and well proportioned. His coat is sleek and short and hard, and lies so close it looks as if he wore sealskin. Generally it is satin black, with tan markings on legs, neck, muzzle, cheeks, and a polka dot of brown above each eye. His tail is docked very short, and his ears are trimmed and set high in erect points. This makes him look always eager and ready for action; and he is!

Watchdog supreme, he can outrun the swiftest fugitive. In every galloping stride his hind legs actually leap ahead of his forelegs. It is an awesome sight to see him overtake and seize his quarry by the wrist and hold on until an officer arrives. Even if fired upon, the dog will not turn tail.

Today, in factories and big stores the world over, he and the watchman stand guard all night. Guns can't hear and they can't smell, and sometimes they jam and don't go off. But Herr Dobermann's Pinscher is surefire.

Yet with all his trigger-action, he is too much the gentleman-detective to bite promiscuously. He has an uncanny sense for discriminating between the innocent and the guilty. The sharpness that Herr Louis wanted is there, and with it a steadfastness and loyalty to his job and his master, even unto death.

Little Die-Hard, the Scottish Terrier

HE HAILS FROM the windy moors of Scotland, this rough-haired fellow with the jaw that says do-or-die. In early times he was bred to "go to earth" and drag foxes, badgers, weasels, and rats from their dens. For each pelt the Scotty's owner was paid a bounty; so what he looked for in his Terrier was a powerful build and a brave spirit.

Nature made this rat-catcher short-legged for his underground work, and grizzled his coat so that in shadowy heather or hedgerow he could hunt unnoticed.

"Earth dogges" is the way King James VI of Scotland described his own Terriers. Being a learned man and a teacher at heart, he liked to explain that the name "terrier" came from the Latin *terra*, meaning "earth."

King James was a clever one with dogs, and a clever one with talk. Whenever he entertained royalty from countries known for their big dogs, he always managed to get in a word about his own wee Scotties.

"Gude gear comes in bittie bundles," he would chuckle. " 'Tis an old Highland saying, that, and it fits our towsy tykes the way a ring fits the finger."

The King was exceedingly proud of his dog Jowler, who was a great ratter and mouser. Often when Jowler swaggered into the banquet hall bearing a rat in his mouth, the King, holding both his sides in laughter, would taunt his cook: "Look, mon! Jowler prefers my stable to your table!"

The world over, the Scotch Terrier answers to names like Tousle or Whiskers. In fact, the more whiskery he is, the more he is admired. Chin and chop whiskers add

much to his dignity, and bushy brows make his button eyes twinkle. For practical purposes, the brows act as watersheds in case of rain and as mudguards when he goes burrowing. The Scotty's coat is bristly, too, much to the annoyance of his enemies. They can never hold on to him. To them he is an elusive fellow, most exasperating!

Today, in dog shows, Scotties are often trimmed and plucked. Then you can see their underwear, which is soft as lamb's wool. But a working Terrier is never plucked, for the needlelike teeth of badgers and rats might tear him to pieces. *His* teeth, by the way, are exceptionally large and tough, larger even than a Collie's! History tells of one celebrated Scotty who had such strong teeth that he is credited with destroying a hundred rats in ten minutes.

As for the Scotty's heart, he is game to the core. He fights his foe face-to-face with stubborn courage, a trait which has earned him the title "Little Die-Hard."

But don't be misled by all this talk of fighting. The Scottish Terrier is a good-natured companion, and a most dependable babysitter. He will let the baby play with the most tantalizing toys—stuffed rabbits and kittens and teddy bears that squeak—and though the noises set him a-quiver, he never snatches the toys away. He just looks on, old and wise in the ways of babies.

Some owners feel that Scotties are born old. From the time they are puppies, they are square-jawed and businesslike. What if their business *is* rats? As King James said, "Is not the work of the exterminator a worthy occupation?"

52

The Siberian Husky

A TEAM OF HUSKIES stands ready in harness, the lead dog in front, the others snapped in by pairs. It is 1925, late January. The place Nenana, a bleak Alaskan village.

The driver is working fast, loading a small package on the sled, wrapping it in furs. The dogs are yipping and yapping in their eagerness to start. It is as if they know the package contains life-saving serum to be rushed to Nome. An epidemic of diphtheria is raging there, and only the serum can halt it.

Over at the airstrip the plane scheduled to carry the package is grounded by storms. But weather is no barrier to the Siberian Huskies. At the command *Mush* they're off, streaking across the snow, leaping over ice hummocks, racing for the sheer joy of it.

Along the trail other teams stand ready. At Shaktolik, the famous driver Seppala waits with his lead dog Togo and a team of twenty. Seppala has a message from Nome: DON'T CUT ACROSS NORTON BAY. HURRICANE WINDS BREAKING UP ICE. But Seppala pays no heed. Going around the bay would mean hours! He cracks his whip, shouts, "Let's go!"

Across the ice Togo feels his way. He knows this shortcut well, but today the ice is buckling, with splinters tearing loose, ripping the pads of his feet. With paws bleeding he and his teammates finish the lap, and a new relay takes over.

Night comes. And morning. And night again. Team after team carries the precious cargo. The wind grows angrier—fifty miles an hour, sixty, then eighty! The temperature falls to fifty below. Gunnar Kasson is the last driver with big black Balto his lead dog.

But let Gunnar tell his own story:

I took the serum at Bluff. The snow was raging. I hitched the dogs. I wanted to get to Point Safety before the trails got impassable.

I stuck to the coast, figuring it would be good going. The wind was howling in from the north, picking up the snow like it was a comb. I didn't know where I was. But Balto sniffed the trail through the snow, pushing ahead.

The sled kept spilling over and I had to untangle the dogs' harness and lift the stuff back and get going again. It was black night. When we got to Point Safety, I mushed right by the road-house. Everything was dark. Balto and the others were jogging steady. I decided to go on instead of waking the next driver for the last twenty miles.

By now the snow had drifted and the air was biting cold. Two dogs began to stiffen up. I made rabbit skin coverings for them, put moccasins on all the dogs. Somehow, at 5:36 on the morning of February second, we staggered into Nome.

A cheering huddle of humanity greeted Gunnar Kasson. But he did not hear. He was pulling ice splinters from Balto's paws while the great dog licked the tears running down his master's beard.

Today in Central Park in New York City, there stands a bigger-than-life statue of a Husky. The inscription reads:

Dedicated to the indomitable spirit of the sled dogs that relayed antitoxin 600 miles over rough ice, through Arctic blizzards, from Nenana to the relief of stricken Nome.

Some say the statue is of Balto, and others say, "No! It is Togo—or Wolf—or Scotty." But what does it matter? Gunnar and Seppala both would say, "It fits them all!"

The Dachshund–Big Enough*

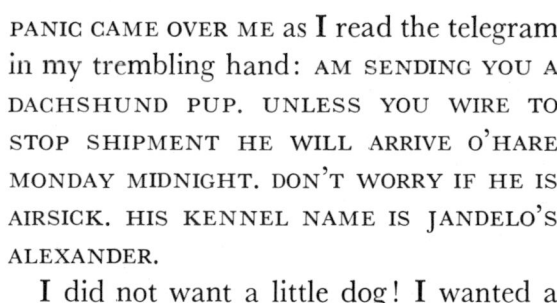

PANIC CAME OVER ME as I read the telegram in my trembling hand: AM SENDING YOU A DACHSHUND PUP. UNLESS YOU WIRE TO STOP SHIPMENT HE WILL ARRIVE O'HARE MONDAY MIDNIGHT. DON'T WORRY IF HE IS AIRSICK. HIS KENNEL NAME IS JANDELO'S ALEXANDER.

I did not want a little dog! I wanted a great big dog—like a Dalmatian, or even a Saint Bernard—one so big that when I sat on the floor before the fire, I could rest my riding boots on his belly without hurting him in the least.

But a Dachshund pup! I could see him now—a caricature of a dog, an animated sausage! I read the telegram again: UNLESS YOU WIRE TO STOP SHIPMENT. . . .

The telephone was at my elbow. Ten little words would keep the Dachshund away. Call Western Union! Do it!

But I seemed under a spell. In my mind I already saw the crate, with the frightened eyes looking out, and the pup not really airsick, just bewildered and lonely for his litter brothers and sisters.

At midnight, when Alexander arrived, he was not bewildered at all. With tail on high, he strutted out of the crate—a gnomelike little fellow, except for his chest, which stuck out like a prizefighter's. He jumped into our car with great swagger. And at the first toll station he made it growlingly clear to the collector that he was our friend and protector.

For good reason my husband had named our place Mole Meadow. Our land was virtually undermined by the burrowing little pests. But even as a pup Alexander declared war on moles. Yapping in excite-ment, he found their winding runs. Then, making a ditch-digger of himself, he shoveled the dirt away with his forepaws, his nose pushing ahead like some pointed plow, until it came upon the enemy.

Mole Meadow is a misnomer now. We haven't seen a mole in so long that I've forgotten what they look like. No, I do remember. They have well-padded feet with powerful claws for digging, just like Alexander's. And they have a pointed muzzle—like his, too. But there the resemblance ends. He is all merry lightheartedness, and they are dark and drab as the tunnels they burrow.

In ridding our place of moles and mice and woodchucks, Alex was carrying on the tradition of his forebears. His family tree goes back to the fifteenth century, to the badger hounds bred by the foresters of Germany. *Dachs* means "badger" in German and *hund* is "dog." Hence the name of this courageous little hunter who is built long and low for burrowing.

In spite of their short legs, Dachshunds can run fast enough to follow the trail of a horse. Always when I went riding, Alex would trot along, tracking our scent even when we galloped out of sight.

On chill autumn nights, after a brisk hour across country, Alex would tear into the house and sprawl in front of the fire, toasting his bones in canine content. When my chores were done, I joined him on the floor, and pulling off my boots, wriggled my toes under his warm body.

"Too small a dog?" my husband often mused with a smile.

No, indeed! Just big enough.

Many Purebreds Make the Mongrel

A FEW YEARS AGO, at the edge of a swamp touching the waters of Green Bay, Wisconsin, there was a drear and dismal dog pound, neither wind- nor rainproof. It housed only a handful of orphaned pups and bedraggled strays who howled their misery night and day. No one cared for them, for their stay at the pound was usually brief. If they were not called for in five days, they were pitilessly put to death, and their bodies carried to a grim black furnace across the road.

The boy Larry, who lived nearby, hated the furnace. To him it was a fire-breathing dragon licking its chops, awaiting its prey.

On his way to fish along the marshy shore, Larry would race past the furnace, scarce breathing, scarce looking. Yet in spite of it all, he found the swamp an exciting place. Wild ducks and geese, marsh hawks, and loons used it for an airport, zooming in for landings, then taking off with a great clatter of wings.

Larry often fished from a tiny footbridge. And while he fished, he looked out over the water and watched the wild, free birds, and he was content. But sometimes a gust of wind brought howlings from the pound and acrid smoke from the furnace. Then his fun was gone. He would gather up his own dog and hold him close.

Larry worried about the caged-up dogs, and often dreamed of them. In his dream he was big and strong, and he strode into the pound wearing seven-league boots. Quickly pulling them off, he filled them to overflowing with little dogs, big dogs, scrawny dogs, fat pups. Then he spirited them away to Never-Never Land, where

eager children claimed them all.

One bleak November day Larry's dream came almost true! The City of Green Bay appointed his father master of the pound. And suddenly Larry was no longer a boy who fished and played in the swamp; he became man-grown overnight.

There was so much to do. The dogs needed help quickly. A part-Collie had a rasping cough which could be distemper. A Pointerlike dog was so scrawny that Larry's father shook his fist at the unknown owner. "That tomfool idiot who starved him! I'd like to try my karate on him."

The boy, listening, felt a sudden pride in his father. "Dad," he said, "we don't *have* to put any of them to death—do we, Dad?"

"That we don't! To my way, every dog has a right to a home." He was stirring up a cough mixture of honey and cherry wine. "We'll cure their ills, son," he said, talking in time with his stirring. "We'll feed 'em, body and soul. Then you'll see! Folks will be standing in line to adopt 'em."

After the sick dogs were tended and the hungry fed, father and son attacked the grime and mildew everywhere. They scrubbed and scoured the cages. They washed the windows and let the sun flow in. They chinked up the cracks in the walls, stuffed gunnysacks around the doors. They kept a fire going in the old pot-bellied stove and put teakettles of water on to boil. Soon steam seeped into every corner of the room, and the half-Collie breathed more easily. As for the ribby Pointer, he was dozing contentedly, head between his paws, next to his tongue-polished feed dish.

When the indoors had been made snug,

Larry and his father began to worry that it would be too warm for the heavy-furred dogs. So they bought lumber and tar paper and built cozy outdoor coops for them. Each one had a vestibule-like entrance, opening to an inner chamber for warmth; and pieces of burlap were tacked over the doorways to keep the winter winds out.

Each morning now Larry was at the pound by sunup, filling the water pans, feeding the dogs, then letting them out for a romp in their runs.

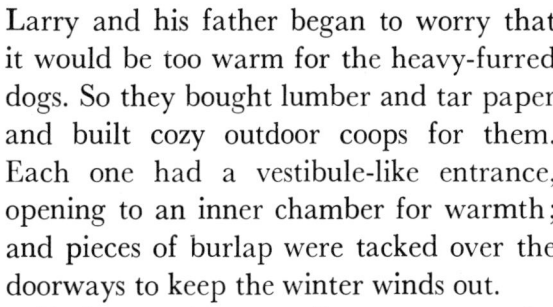

But one mongrel was a problem dog. She refused to leave her cage. When Larry opened it, her lip curled up over her fangs and the growl in her throat was menacing.

Larry felt a deep hurt that any creature could mistrust him. He named the stubborn one Meanie-Muggs, and determined to make her a friend. Whenever he went by her cage, he spoke her name softly. "You're the meanie one," he would say, his voice gentle with reproof. "But we'll change that. Why, anyone can see you've got Terrier blood, which tells me you're a fine mouser. And that Bulldog chest of yours shows you've got spunk. Why, you must have lots of purebred blood."

One evening after school, Larry brought Muggs a toy mouse. For a long time she held it in her mouth, with only the tail sticking out. Who could growl with a mouthful of mouse? Not Muggs.

It took weeks of coaxing, however, before she ventured out of her cage. When at last she did, it was such fun that she didn't want to go back. Cunningly, she figured a way to make the recess last longer. Instead of meekly following the other dogs to their cages when the hour of play was up, she hid behind a trash barrel where she had stashed her mouse. Larry ignored her for a while and then turned her naughtiness into a game of hide-and-seek. In the end he would swoop her up and carry her to her cage as if she were some helpless child. Shyly at first, she dabbed at his cheek with her tongue; then her tail did a wild tattoo against his ribs.

There was magic in the way Muggs blossomed. She soon became a "trusty" with special privileges. When Larry made his rounds of the restaurants to collect meat scraps and knuckle bones, she was allowed to go along for the ride. Balancing herself on his bicycle, she loved the feel of the wind streaming past her face. The scent of the bones in the basket tickled her nose. But she would never touch one until Larry gave the signal.

Muggs became an active worker, too. She taught herself to climb up the ladder into the loft, where she rid the place of real mice. And she sounded the alarm whenever foxes threatened the eggs of ducks and geese nesting close to the pound. And she became expert at mothering frightened new dogs.

The magic did not end with Muggs. Before the year was up, the whole pound was transformed. When winter came again, and winds raged and snow drifted around the building, the big room was a friendly place—teakettle whistling, the father's pencil scratching at his reports, the dogs snoring or howling off-key with the new radio, and Larry hammering away at more cages.

To his great delight the pound was be-

coming known as a refuge for homeless, friendless dogs instead of an exterminator. Some days the phone rang incessantly:

"Come get a mangy mutt running loose on our street and upsetting garbage cans."

"Please pick up a little abandoned dog who's been sitting for days at the Jean Nicolet statue."

"Come get a bitch and her five mongrel pups from under our front porch."

All these were taken in and made welcome, even the runtiest. "Somebody will want him," the father insisted. And somebody always did. "Half-pint," an undersized yapper, lived a whole year at the pound before a loving grandmother saw the goodness in his homely face and tucked him into a child's Christmas stocking. In his adopted home Half-pint learned to be discreet about barking and became a bustling partner in the business of raising a small child.

Larry's father was very firm in this matter of adoption. Each prospect was questioned as carefully as a foster parent asking for a baby. And each adoption was followed up to make certain that the dog had adjusted to his new home. If he appeared to be mistreated or unhappy, he was promptly taken back to the pound, where wild barks of joy and frantic tails would welcome the returning fellow! Larry was as joyful as the dogs.

"We need more old-timers like Muggs, don't we, Dad, to help train the scared newcomers."

The father smiled, secretly happy at the boy's wisdom. "You're right, Larry. To my way, each dog has a place waiting for him. Here we have purebreds and mongrels to fit every need; we have herders and hunters, burrowers and retrievers, guard dogs and just plain footwarmers."

"And even if they're mostly mongrels," Larry said, "I like 'em all!"

"Why, there's nothing to sneer at in mongrels, son. I once read an article by a man named Terhune, a real dog man. And he said there couldn't be a worse mistake than to sneer at the mongrel. Why, in his mind, the mongrel had more cleverness, more stamina, and sometimes more beauty than a purebred. And the only shame, he said, is the owner's failure to bring out his many fine traits."

"He's right, Dad."

"And think about this, Larry. Does the Red Cross worry about the ancestry of their dogs? Does the Army Medical Corps? Do circus trainers?

"No!" the father barked, sounding exactly like one of his dogs. Then his voice quieted. "You see, it's the mixed-up background that often gives a pup the best qualities of several breeds. Makes him smart and healthy."

"Hey, Dad! I just thought of something! Mongrels are a mixture like us! They're Americans!"

And in full agreement there stood Muggs, winking a knowing eye at her friends and thumping her tail in happiness.

For their help the author is grateful to:

ADVISER
Miss Emmeline Andruskevicz

AMERICAN FIELD, THE (magazine)
William F. Brown, *editor*

AMERICAN FOX TERRIER CLUB
J. W. Smith, *secretary*

AMERICAN KENNEL CLUB, INC.
Miss Beatrice E. Peterson, *librarian*

AMERICAN POMERANIAN CLUB
Miss Joy Brewster, *secretary*

AMERICAN SPANIEL CLUB
Mrs. Margaret M. Ciezkowski, *secretary*

BOXER BREEDER AND OBEDIENCE JUDGE
Mrs. Lorraine C. Meyer
My-R Kennels

BOXER FANCIER
Rudy Docky, Polack Brothers Circus

BULLDOG CLUB OF AMERICA
Callan S. Riggs, *secretary*

CHIHUAHUA FANCIER
Mrs. Walter P. Chrysler

COLLIE CLUB OF AMERICA, INC.
John Honig, *secretary*

ENGLISH SPRINGER SPANIEL FIELD
TRIAL ASSOCIATION, INC.
Mrs. Evelyn Monte, *secretary*

FOX TERRIER FANCIER
Anthony Welling
Cleveland Police Department

GERMAN SHEPHERD DOG CLUB OF
AMERICA, INC.
Miss Blanche L. Beisswenger, *secretary*

GREAT DANE FANCIER
Mrs. Elizabeth Whitney Tippett

HOUNDS AND HUNTING (magazine)
I. W. Carrel, *editor*

LABRADOR RETRIEVER CLUB, INC.
William K. Laughlin, *secretary*

MONGREL FANCIERS
Clarence and Larry Verheyden

NATIONAL BEAGLE CLUB
Morgan Wing, Jr., *secretary*

PEKINGESE FANCIER
Miss Frances J. Carter

POODLE CLUB OF AMERICA
F. P. Fretwell, *secretary*

SAINT BERNARD CLUB OF AMERICA
Mrs. William Beyer, *assistant to the
secretary*

SCOTTISH TERRIER FANCIER
Mrs. Earl Vogt

SIBERIAN HUSKY BREEDER AND JUDGE
Mrs. Nicholas A. Demidoff
Monadnock Kennels

For the Cocker Spaniel incident, credit
is due Miss Violet Stefanich and to
the publication *Our Dumb Animals*.

64